CURRICULUM AND EVALUATION
S T A N D A R D S
FOR SCHOOL MATHEMATICS
ADDENDA SERIES, GRADES K–6

F O U R T H - G R A D E   B O O K

Grace Burton

Douglas Clements

Terrence Coburn

John Del Grande

John Firkins

Jeane Joyner

Miriam A. Leiva

Mary M. Lindquist

Lorna Morrow

Miriam A. Leiva, Series Editor

NATIONAL COUNCIL OF
TEACHERS OF MATHEMATICS

Copyright © 1992 by
THE NATIONAL COUNCIL OF TEACHERS OF MATHEMATICS, INC.
1906 Association Drive, Reston, Virginia 22091-1593
All rights reserved

Third printing 1992

Library of Congress Cataloging-in-Publication Data:

Fourth-grade book / Grace Burton ... [et al.].
      p.   cm. — (Curriculum and evaluation standards for school
   mathematics addenda series. Grades K–6)
     Includes bibliographical references.
     ISBN 0-87353-314-3: $11.00
     1. Mathematics—Study and teaching (Elementary)   I. Burton,
Grace M.   II. National Council of Teachers of Mathematics.
III. Series.
QA135.5.F635   1991 2
372.7—dc20   91-47648
                                                    QA   CIP
                                                    135.5
                                                    .F635
                                                    1992

Photograph is by Patricia Fisher; artwork is by Lynn Gohman and Don Christian.

The publications of the National Council of Teachers of Mathematics present a variety of viewpoints. The views expressed or implied in this publication, unless otherwise noted, should not be interpreted as official positions of the Council.

Printed in the United States of America

FOREWORD

The *Curriculum and Evaluation Standards for School Mathematics* (NCTM 1989a) describes a framework for revising and strengthening school mathematics. This visionary document provides a set of guidelines for K–12 mathematics curricula and for evaluating both the mathematics curriculum and students' progress. It not only addresses what mathematics students should learn but also how they should learn it.

As the document was being developed, it became apparent that supporting publications would be needed to interpret and illustrate how the vision could be translated realistically into classroom practices. A Task Force on the Addenda to the Curriculum and Evaluation Standards for School Mathematics, chaired by Thomas Rowan and composed of Joan Duea, Christian Hirsch, Marie Jernigan, and Richard Lodholz, was appointed by Shirley Frye, then NCTM president. The Task Force's recommendations on the scope and nature of the supporting publications were submitted to the Educational Materials Committee, which subsequently framed the Addenda Project.

Central to the Addenda Project was the formation of three writing teams—consisting of classroom teachers, mathematics supervisors, and university mathematics educators—to prepare a series of publications, the Addenda Series, targeted at mathematics instruction in grades K–6, 5–8, and 9–12. The purpose of the series is to clarify and illustrate the message of the *Curriculum and Evaluation Standards*. The underlying themes of problem solving, reasoning, communication, and connections are woven throughout the materials, as is the view of assessment as a means of guiding instruction. Activities have been field tested by teachers to ensure that they reflect the realities of today's classrooms.

It is envisioned that the Addenda Series will be a source of ideas by teachers as they begin to implement the recommendations in the NCTM *Curriculum and Evaluation Standards*. Individual volumes in the series are appropriate for in-service programs and for preservice courses in teacher education programs.

A project of this magnitude required the efforts and talents of many people over an extended time. Sincerest appreciation is extended to the authors and the editor and to the following teachers who played key roles in developing, revising, and trying out the materials for the *Fourth Grade Book:* Angela C. Gardner, Debra Latozas, and Carolyn Lennon. Finally, this project would not have materialized without the outstanding technical support supplied by Cynthia Rosso and the NCTM publications staff.

Bonnie H. Litwiller
Addenda Project Coordinator

PREFACE

Something exciting is happening in many elementary school classrooms! A vision of an innovative mathematics program is coming alive. There *is* a shift in emphasis in the teaching and learning of mathematics. Teachers are encouraging children to investigate, discuss, question, and verify. They are focusing on explorations and dialogues. They are using various strategies to assess students' progress. They are making mathematics accessible to all children while exposing them to the value and the beauty of mathematics. Teachers and students are excited, and their enthusiasm is contagious. You can *catch it* when you hear children confidently explaining their solutions to the class, when you see them modeling problems with manipulatives, and when you observe them using a variety of methods and materials to arrive at answers. Some children are working with paper and pencil or with calculators; others are sharpening their estimation and mental math skills. There is noise in these classrooms—the sounds of students actively participating in the class and constructing their own knowledge through experiences that will give them confidence in their own abilities and make them mathematically powerful.

> I remember my own experiences in mathematics in elementary school. The classroom was quiet; all you could hear was the movement of pencils across sheets of paper and an occasional comment from the teacher. I was often bored; work was done in silent isolation, rules were memorized, and many routine problems were worked using rules few of us understood. Mathematics didn't always make sense. It was something that you did in school, mostly with numbers, and that you didn't need outside the classroom.
>
> "Why are we doing this?" my friend whispered.
>
> "Because it's in the book," I replied.
>
> "Do it this way," the teacher would explain while writing another problem on the chalkboard. "When you finish, work the next ten problems in the book."

We must go beyond how we were taught and teach how we wish we had been taught. We must bring to life a vision of what a mathematics classroom should be.

Rationale for Change

These are challenging times for you, the teachers of elementary school mathematics, and for your students. Major reforms in school mathematics are advocated in reports that call for changes in the curriculum, in student and program evaluations, in instruction, and in the classroom environment. These reforms are prompted by the changing needs of our society, which demand that all students become mathematically literate to function effectively in a technological world. A richer mathematics program is also supported by an explosion of new mathematical knowledge—more mathematics has been created in this century than in all our previous history. Research studies on teaching and learning, with emphasis on *how children learn mathematics,* have had a significant impact on current practices and strengthen the case for reform. Advances in technology also dictate changes in content and teaching.

Our students, the citizens of tomorrow, need to learn not only *more* mathematics but also mathematics that is broader in scope. They must have a strong academic foundation to enable them to expand their knowledge, to interpret information, to make reasonable decisions, and to solve increasingly complex problems using various approaches and tools, including calculators and computers. Mathematics instruction must reflect and implement these revised educational goals and increased expectations.

The blueprint for reform is the *Curriculum and Evaluation Standards for School Mathematics* (National Council of Teachers of Mathematics 1989a), which identifies a set of standards for the mathematics curriculum in grades K–12 as well as standards for evaluating the quality of programs and students' performance. The *Curriculum and Evaluation Standards* sets forth a bold vision of what mathematics education in grades K–12 should be and describes how mathematics classrooms can fit the vision.

Mathematics as Sense Making

In the past, mathematics classrooms were dominated by instruction and performance of rote procedures "to get the right answer." The *Curriculum and Evaluation Standards* supports the view of school mathematics as a sense-making experience encompassing a wide range of content, instructional approaches, and evaluation techniques.

Four standards are closely woven into content and instruction: mathematics as problem solving, mathematics as communication, mathematics as reasoning, and mathematical connections. These strands are common themes that support all other standards throughout all grade levels.

A primary goal for the study of mathematics is to give children experiences that promote the ability *to solve problems* and that build mathematics from situations generated within the context of everyday experiences. Students are also expected *to make conjectures and conclusions* and *to discuss their reasoning* in words, both written and spoken; with pictures, graphs, and charts; and with manipulatives. Moreover, students learn *to value mathematics* when they *make connections* between topics in mathematics, between the concrete and the abstract, between concepts and skills, and between mathematics and other areas in the curriculum.

The Changing Roles of Students

Previous efforts to reform school mathematics focused primarily on the curriculum; the *Curriculum and Evaluation Standards* also deals with other factors—in particular, students—that affect and are affected by reforms. The role of students is redirected from passive recipients to active participants, from isolated workers to team members, from listeners to investigators and reporters, and from timid followers to intrepid explorers and risk takers. They are asked to develop, discuss, create, model, validate, and investigate to learn mathematics.

Many people, including students, believe that mathematics is for the privileged few. It is time to dispel that myth. All children, regardless of sex, socioeconomic background, language, race, or ethnic origin, can and must succeed in school mathematics. With proper instruction, encouragement, and high expectations, *all* students can do mathematics.

Your Role in Implementing the Standards

All elementary school teachers are teachers of mathematics. Thus, your role is to build your students' self-confidence and nurture their natural curiosity; to challenge them with rich problems through which they will learn to value mathematics and appreciate the order and beauty of mathematics; to provide them with a strong foundation for further study; and to encourage their mathematical ability and power.

The elementary school years are crucial in a child's cognitive and affective development, and you are the central figure. You structure class-

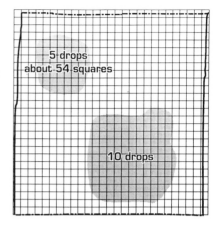

We did an experiment to find out which brand of paper towels was the most absorbent. We measured the wet areas by counting squares on a grid.

My story quilt is about Mexico. Dad helped me draw the map.

We made a clock that
Mr. Brown called a sundial.
Fourth grade is fun.

We colored our circle
pictures. Mom thought it
was art, but it was math!

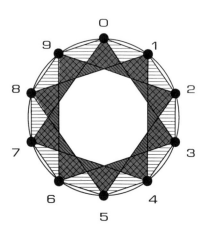

Can you guess my rule?

3	5
4	7
5	9

The second number is twice the first, minus 1.

room experiences to implement the curriculum and create a supportive environment for learning to take place. In most activities you are the guide, the coach, the facilitator, and the instigator of mathematical explorations.

♦ You give children the gift of self-confidence. Through your careful grouping, astute questions, appropriate tasks, and realistic expectations, each student can experience success.

♦ Long after they forget childhood events, your students will remember you. Your excitement and interest permeate the room and stimulate their appreciation for mathematics.

♦ Through your classroom practices, you promote mathematical thinking, reasoning, and understanding.

♦ You lay the foundation on which further study will take place. You give students multiple strategies and tools to solve problems. The questions you ask and the problems you pose can capture your students' imagination, arouse their curiosity, and encourage their creativity.

♦ You facilitate the building of their knowledge by giving them interesting problems to solve, which leads to the development of concepts and important mathematical ideas.

♦ Rules, algorithms, and formulas emerge from student explorations guided by you, the teacher of mathematics.

Instructional Tools and the Standards

In order to implement the curriculum envisioned in the *Curriculum and Evaluation Standards,* we must carefully select and creatively use instructional tools. The textbook is only one of many important teaching resources. Children's development of concepts is fostered by their extensive use of physical materials to represent and describe mathematical ideas.

Calculators and computers are essential instructional tools at all levels. Through the appropriate use of these tools, students are able to solve realistic problems, investigate patterns, explore procedures, and focus on the steps to solve problems instead of on tedious computations.

Implementing the Evaluation Standards

Evaluation must be an integral part of teaching. A primary component of instruction is an ongoing assessment of what goes on in our classrooms. This information helps us make decisions about what we teach and how we teach it, about students' progress and feelings, and about our mathematics program.

The *Curriculum and Evaluation Standards* advocates many changes in curriculum, in instruction, and in the roles of students and teachers. None of these changes are more important than those related to evaluation. We must learn to use a variety of assessment instruments and not depend on pencil-and-paper tests alone. Tools such as observations, interviews, projects, reports, portfolios, diaries, and tests provide a more complete picture of what children understand and are able to use. Knowing what questions to ask is a skill we must develop.

When we test, we send a message about what we think is important. Because we encourage reasoning and communicating mathematically, we practice these skills. Because manipulatives and calculators are valuable tools for learning, we promote their use in the classroom. Because we want children to experience cooperative problem solving, we provide opportunities for group activities. *Not only must we evaluate what we want children to learn, but also how we want them to learn it.*

You and This Book

This booklet is part of the Curriculum and Evaluation for School Mathematics Addenda Series, Grades K–6. This series was designed to illustrate the standards and to help you translate them into classroom practice through—

♦ sample lessons and discussions that focus on the development of concepts;

♦ activities that connect models and manipulatives with concepts and with mathematical representations;

♦ problems that exemplify the use and integration of technology;

♦ teaching strategies that promote students' reasoning;

♦ approaches to evaluate students' progress;

♦ techniques to improve instruction.

In this booklet, both traditional and new topics are explored in four areas: Patterns, Number Sense and Operations, Making Sense of Data, and Geometry and Spatial Sense.

You will find classic fourth-grade activities that have been infused with an investigative flavor. These experiences include investigating lines of symmetry using Logo; exploring angles with manipulatives and with the computer; studying shadows and the foundation of projective geometry; designing and conducting experiments that involve collecting, organizing, and interpreting data; developing estimation strategies in a variety of activities; using patterns to solve problems and to make conjectures; validating rules and functions; and using calculators to explore numerical patterns, decimal fractions, and negative numbers. You will also encounter a variety of problems and questions to explore with your fourth graders. Margin notes give you additional information on the activities and on such topics as student self-confidence, evaluation, and grouping. Connections to science, language arts, social studies, and other areas in the curriculum are made throughout. Supporting statements from the *Curriculum and Evaluation Standards* appear as margin notes.

Change is an ongoing process that takes time and courage. It is not easy to go beyond comfort and security to try new things. As you use this book, pick and choose at will, and sample alternative approaches and ideas for instruction and assessment. Savor the freedom of change. All the documents in the world will not effect change in the classrooms; *only you can.*

The Challenge and the Vision

"I wonder why...?"

"What would happen if...?"   "Tell me about your pattern."

"Can you do it another way?"   "Our group has a different solution."

These inviting words give students the freedom to be creative, the confidence to solve problems, and the power to do mathematics. When you give your students the opportunity to construct their own knowledge, you are opening the doors of mathematics to *all* young learners.

This is the challenge. This is the vision.

Miriam A. Leiva, Editor
K–6 Addenda Series

The answer is 36. What is the question?

How many cents are in 1 quarter, 1 dime, and 1 penny?

How many pegs are on the geoboard?

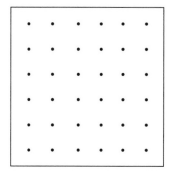

I colored 4/8 of the square. Then I folded it and found that my picture had two lines of symmetry.

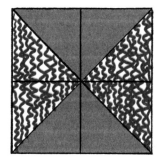

How much water might Columbus have carried for his trip across the Atlantic?

BIBLIOGRAPHY

National Council of Teachers of Mathematics. Curriculum and Evaluation Standards for
   School Mathematics Addenda Series, Grades K–6, edited by Miriam A. Leiva. Reston,
   Va.: The Council, 1991.

_____. Curriculum and Evaluation Standards for School Mathematics Addenda Series,
   Grades 5–8, edited by Frances R. Curcio. Reston, Va.: The Council, 1991.

_____. Curriculum and Evaluation Standards for School Mathematics Addenda Series,
   Grades 9–12, edited by Christian R. Hirsch. Reston, Va.: The Council, 1991.

_____. Curriculum and Evaluation Standards for School Mathematics. Reston, Va.: The
   Council, 1989a.

_____. New Directions for Elementary School Mathematics. 1989 Yearbook of the
   National Council of Teachers of Mathematics. Edited by Paul Trafton. Reston, Va.: The
   Council, 1989b.

_____. Professional Standards for Teaching Mathematics. Reston, Va.: The Council,
   1991.

National Research Council. Everybody Counts: A Report to the Nation on the Future of
   Mathematics Education. Washington, D.C.: National Academy Press, 1989.

O'Brien, Thomas C. The King's Rule. Pleasantville, N.Y.: Sunburst Communications, Inc.,
   1985. Computer software.

ACKNOWLEDGMENTS

At a time when the mathematics community was looking for directions
on implementing the Curriculum and Evaluation Standards for School
Mathematics, a group of dedicated professionals agreed to serve on the
NCTM Elementary Addenda Project.

The task of editing and writing for this series has been challenging
and rewarding. Selecting, testing, writing, and editing, as we attempted
to translate the message of the Standards into classroom practices,
proved to be a monumental and ambitious task. It could not have been
done without the dedication and hard work of the authors, the teachers
who reviewed and field tested the activities, and the editorial team.

My appreciation is extended to the main authors for each topic:

Grace Burton	Number Sense and Operations
Terrence Coburn	Patterns
John Del Grande and Lorna Morrow	Geometry and Spatial Sense
Mary M. Lindquist	Making Sense of Data

Our colleagues in the classrooms, Angela Gardner, Debra Latozas, and
Carolyn Lennon, are thanked for giving us the unique perspective of
teachers and children.

A special note of gratitude is owed to the individuals who served both as
writers and as the editorial panel: Douglas Clements, John Firkins, and
Jeane Joyner.

The editor also gratefully acknowledges the strong support of Bonnie
Litwiller, Coordinator of the Addenda Project, and the assistance of
Cynthia Rosso and the NCTM production staff for their guidance and
help through the process of planning and producing this series of books.

The greatest reward for all who have contributed to this effort will be
the knowledge that the ideas presented here have been implemented in
elementary school classrooms, that these ideas have made realities out
of visions, and that they have fostered improved mathematics programs
for all children.

Miriam A. Leiva

PATTERNS

The study of patterns affords students an opportunity to make conjectures about relationships. Through multiple experiences, students learn that it is important to investigate a pattern in an organized and systematic way. By continuing to provide a broad variety of opportunities to explore and use patterns, we help students move from a basic recognition of patterns to a more sophisticated use of patterns as a problem-solving strategy. In other words, we move from teaching *about* patterns to teaching *with* patterns.

In third grade, children may have explored patterns on the hundreds chart. Many fourth graders will be able to generalize and verbalize number patterns as part of small-group explorations and class discussions. For example, on the hundreds chart, 9, 18, 27, 36, 45, 54, 63, 72, 81, 90,…show a pattern that may be described in many different ways. The units digit in each succeeding number decreases by 1 and the tens digit increases by 1. The sum of the digits is always 9. The numbers, when covered by cubes, make diagonal stripes on the board so we can visually predict the numbers in the pattern.

Students previously may have written numerical descriptions of growing patterns as a stage in learning to generalize a rule for a pattern. Some fourth-grade children may be able to write a mathematical expression or a sentence describing the pattern they see. To answer "How many marbles in each term?" a student might reply, "The pattern is growing so that in each term, the array has one more row and one more column."

Organizing data on a pattern in a table helps students identify its structure and describe it symbolically. (NCTM 1989a, p. 61)

1	2	3	4	5	6	7	8	9	10
11	12	13	14	15	16	17	18	19	20
21	22	23	24	25	26	27	28	29	30
31	32	33	34	35	36	37	38	39	40
41	42	43	44	45	46	47	48	49	50
51	52	53	54	55	56	57	58	59	60
61	62	63	64	65	66	67	68	69	70
71	72	73	74	75	76	77	78	79	80
81	82	83	84	85	86	87	88	89	90
91	92	93	94	95	96	97	98	99	100

Term	1	2	3	4
Number of marbles	1 x 2	2 x 3	3 x 4	?

Patterns can furnish a review of the multiplication facts while deepening students' understanding of multiples. The geometric designs resulting from patterns of multiples intrigue students. They also help students generate conjectures about numerical relationships.

As children work on basic facts, encourage them to look for patterns and relationships.

What patterns can you find in the multiples of 6? Can you find a pattern in the multiples of 2, 4, and 8?

What are the differences and similarities among these patterns?

Is 239 a multiple of 6? How do you know?

If a number is a multiple of 6, is it a multiple of 2? Of 4?

What numbers are multiples of 2, 4, 6, and 8?

0 x 2 = **0**	0 x 4 = **0**	0 x 6 = **0**	0 x 8 = **0**
1 x 2 = **2**	1 x 4 = **4**	1 x 6 = **6**	1 x 8 = **8**
2 x 2 = **4**	2 x 4 = **8**	2 x 6 = 12	2 x 8 = 16
3 x 2 = **6**	3 x 4 = 12	3 x 6 = 18	3 x 8 = 24
4 x 2 = **8**	4 x 4 = 16	4 x 6 = 24	4 x 8 = 32
5 x 2 = 10	5 x 4 = 20	5 x 6 = 30	5 x 8 = 40
6 x 2 = 12	6 x 4 = 24	6 x 6 = 36	6 x 8 = 48
7 x 2 = 14	7 x 4 = 28	7 x 6 = 42	7 x 8 = 56
8 x 2 = 16	8 x 4 = 32	8 x 6 = 48	8 x 8 = 64
9 x 2 = 18	9 x 4 = 36	9 x 6 = 54	9 x 8 = 72

Two activities in this section deepen children's understanding of the multiplication facts. The counting rectangles activity illustrates the impor-

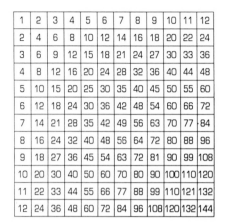

tance of being organized and using a table as part of studying a pattern. Guess My Rule is a classic activity for encouraging children to generalize from a pattern. Activities such as these help children see the power of patterns.

MULTIPLICATION TABLE PATTERNS

Get ready. The purpose of this activity is to have children investigate patterns of multiples in a multiplication table.

This activity provides a good review of the multiplication facts. You will need eleven copies of the 12 × 12 multiplication table (p. 7) for each student group and copies for use on the overhead projector. Using a 12s table gives more variety in patterns than using a 10s table. Calculators will help children focus on the patterns without getting slowed down by the computations. Students need pens or crayons for coloring the tables. If possible, have them use a different color for each number 2 through 12. Transparent colored chips work well on the overhead projector. Counters are useful for children at their desks.

Time invested in group dis-cussions helps all students understand the tasks and gives the teacher an oppor-tunity to assess students' knowledge as they respond to questions.

Get going. As a class, list and discuss the multiples of 6. On the over-head transparency, color or cover each multiple on the multiplication table and discuss the patterns. Ask each group to color separate tables for the multiples of 2, 3, 4, 5, 7, 8, 9, 10, 11, and 12. If counters are available, the children can use them to find the pattern before coloring. The students may divide among their group the tasks of listing the multi-ples and coloring the tables. Allow time for the groups to investigate their completed tables. Encourage them to look for distinct as well as similar patterns. Ask the groups to provide a written statement describ-ing their findings. Encourage the students to reflect on what they have seen, clarify their thinking, and be prepared to share their thoughts.

When the groups come back together, ask the students to report on what they discovered. You may need to facilitate the discussion with questions:

Are there any tables with the same pattern?

Is there anything similar between the tables?

Do you see a difference between the tables with multiples of odd num-bers and the tables with even multiples?

Display the multiplication tables that the students have colored and have the class determine which multiples, 2 through 12, each represents.

How did you figure that out?

Ask questions about a table pattern for a specific multiple. For example, focus attention on the table for 6, in which every third number in the row for 2 is shaded.

Who can tell me why?

Which rows are completely shaded? Why?

There are only two numbers shaded in the row for 5. Why?

Ask the students to predict the patterns of other tables.

What do you think the pattern would be for the table of 13 or 17? Why do you think so?

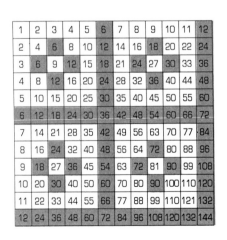

Keep going. Ask the students,

If you were to fold the table along the diagonal—from top left to bottom right—what do you notice?

Challenge pairs of students to find two new patterns on the multiplication table, describing and explaining them in a written report.

Challenge the students to construct other multiplication tables. For example, the 23s table shows us that 2 × 23 is 4 tens and 6 ones, or 46; 3 × 23 is 6 tens and 9 ones, or 69; 4 × 23 is 8 tens and 12 ones, or 92; and 5 × 23 is 10 tens and 15 ones, or 115. In like manner, we can quickly figure that 3 × 32 is 96 and 5 × 32 is 15 tens and 10 ones, or 160.

		Tens	Ones
	×	2	3
	1	2	3
	2	4	6
	3	6	9
	4	8	12
	5	10	15

GOING IN CIRCLES

Get ready. The purpose of this activity is to have children make designs while exploring the relationships between the ones digit of the multiples of a number and the number itself. Each geometric design relates to a particular pattern of ones digits.

You will need copies of the Circle Patterns blackline master (p. 8), pencils, crayons, and straightedges. Reproduce three copies of the blackline master for each small group.

Get going. Have the students complete the first table with the multiples of 7 and highlight the ones digit in each multiple as illustrated. The completed table should look like this:

0	1	2	3	4	5	6	7	8	9	10	11	12
0	7	14	21	28	35	42	49	56	63	70	77	84

Have the students list the circled digits and extend the table until they notice that the number pattern repeats.

Guide the students in connecting the points on the circle according to the numbers in the repeating pattern. For the 7 pattern, start with point 0 and draw a straight line to point 7. Connect point 7 to point 4, point 4 to point 1, and so on, until you connect back to the starting point.

Can you describe the figure that we have created?

Have the groups develop tables and circle patterns for other sets of multiplication facts: 2, 3, 4, 6, 8, 9. Encourage them to color their designs.

Keep going. Allow the students time to compare their circle patterns.

How can you describe the designs?

Encourage the students to use geometric concepts such as angles, sides, and triangles to describe their designs.

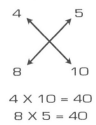

"I discovered that for four numbers in a square, the products of the numbers on the diagonals are equal."

4 X 10 = 40
8 X 5 = 40

"When I looked at two rows together, I saw equivalent fractions. The first and second rows have 1/2, 2/4, 3/6, and so on. The second and fifth rows have 2/5, 4/10, and so on. It works for any two rows!"

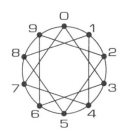

This circle graph illustrates the ones digits in the multiplication tables for 7 or 3.

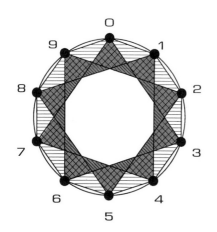

Patterns for 3 and 9

Every classroom will have at least one computer available at all times for demonstrations and student use. Additional computers should be available for individual, small-group, and whole-class use. (NCTM 1989a, p. 68)

If your students have had little experience with this activity, begin with easy rules that relate two numbers. Give the number pairs and challenge them to guess your rule:

1	*2*
2	*4*
3	*6*

Rule: The second number is two times the first number.

Are any of the circle designs the same? Why? [Some are the same, but some are different. For example, the circles for 6 and 4 will look like 5-pointed stars.]

Why are some of the circle patterns different? [The number patterns are different.]

What do you think the pattern is for 11? Why? What do you think the pattern is for 100? For 32? Why?

Which tables give you a semicircle? Is there more than one table that would do so?

Which tables give you a point on the circle?

There is an infinite number of counting numbers. Is there an infinite number of circle patterns?

Make colorful decorations for your class by having students make several patterns on the same circle, using a different color for each sequence of multiples. This connects art to mathematics.

WHAT'S MY RULE?

Get ready. The purpose of this activity is to help students recognize number patterns and test their conjectures. Students solve number riddles by guessing the rules that apply to sets of three numbers. The focus is on describing a pattern both orally and in writing.

You can do this activity with or without a computer. To use the computer, you will need software that generates numerical patterns (such as the King's Rule [O'Brien 1985]) and, ideally, a display device for the overhead projector or a large-screen monitor. If these materials are not available, a similar activity can be conducted at the chalkboard.

Get going. Explain to the class that the goal of the activity is to guess a rule that you have made up. The rule generates number triples. Think of a rule and write on the chalkboard three numbers related by the rule. For example, if your rule is "the third number is the product of the first two," write this sequence of numbers: 3 5 15. The students give three numbers that they think satisfy the rule. Respond yes or no and keep track of their guesses and your responses on a chart as shown below.

Attempt	Guess			Response
1	1	2	3	Yes
2	12	11	10	No
3	4	5	6	Yes
4	10	11	12	Yes

Rule: Each number is 1 more than the previous number.

Attempt	Guess			Response
1	70	21	7	Yes
2	7	77	17	No
3	3	6	9	No
4	35	42	56	Yes

Rule: All numbers are multiples of 7.

The class continues to name triples and to receive your feedback. When the students think they are ready to guess the rule, give them several triples. They must indicate whether or not the numbers satisfy the rule and describe the rule.

Keep going. Have small groups of students play the game. Let individual students invent their own rules and be rule makers for further class games at the chalkboard. Join the game and see if you can guess the students' rule. Students are delighted when a teacher plays along. Some possibilities for rules follow:

1. The third number is the sum of the first two:

4	7	11
8	2	10

2. The first two numbers are even and the third is always odd:

4	6	7
8	2	5

3. The second number is greater than the sum of the first and third numbers:

2	9	6
10	30	14

The children might also write their own rules and be the rule maker for a partner.

Have the students create their own What's My Rule? bulletin boards. Students could make displays that include geometric as well as numeric patterns.

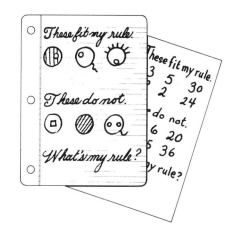

HOW MANY RECTANGLES DO YOU SEE?

Get ready. The purpose of this activity is to help students be organized and systematic observers as they record data related to patterns.

Get going. Draw a 3-rectangle on the chalkboard.

How many rectangles do you see?

Some children will reply that there are three rectangles; others will say that there are more than three. Help them to see and count the total number of rectangles. Refer to the drawing as a 3-rectangle because it is made from three small rectangles (three 1-rectangles).

Draw a 4-rectangle and give the class some time to count the total number of different-sized rectangles in a 4-rectangle.

How many 1-rectangles are there in a 4-rectangle? How many 3-rectangles? Show me.

Guide the class in organizing their information into a table.

3-rectangle

A 3-rectangle has—

3 rectangles this size:

2 rectangles this size:

1 rectangle this size:

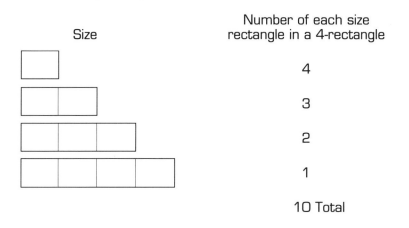

Size	Number of each size rectangle in a 4-rectangle
	4
	3
	2
	1
	10 Total

Fourth grade is not too early to ask students to look for patterns in tables horizontally as well as vertically. As they try to find the relationship of the total number of rectangles in consecutive terms, they might discover a relation–ship between the type of rectangle and its total.

(In a 4-rectangle there are 10 rectangles—1 + 2 + 3 + 4 = 10.)

Type of large rectangle	Total number of different-sized rectangles
1-rectangle	1
2-rectangle	3
3-rectangle	6
4-rectangle	10
5-rectangle	15
6-rectangle	21

With the class, make a table that records the total number of different-sized rectangles in each large rectangle. Enter the data for a 4-rectangle and a 3-rectangle. Ask the children to fill in the total number of rect-angles for the remainder of the table and to look for patterns.

What patterns can you find in the table? [For example, the total number of rectangles for a 4-rectangle drawing is 4 more rectangles than for a 3-rectangle drawing. The total number of rectangles for a 5-rectangle is 5 more than for a 4-rectangle, and so on.]

How many rectangles will there be in a 7-rectangle? [21 + 7, or 28]

If there are 210 rectangles in a 20-rectangle, how many will be in a 19-rectangle? [210 – 20, or 190] *In an 18-rectangle?* [171]

If there are 66 rectangles altogether, what kind of rectangle [i.e., n-rectangle] do we have? [11]

Discuss the idea that being organized and systematic was helpful in seeing a pattern and becoming confident about counting the rectangles in the picture.

Keep going. Engage the students in solving other problems that require organization and pattern recognition.

Ask the students to work in groups to find all the squares whose sides are parallel to the sides of a geoboard as illustrated. They may use grid paper.

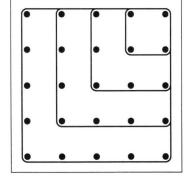

Have them identify the different-sized squares. [1 cm × 1 cm, 2 cm × 2 cm, 3 cm × 3 cm, 4 cm × 4 cm] Ask the students to find out all they can about these nonslanted squares.

Discuss the students' findings. Have each group explain their method of labeling, counting, looking for patterns, and so on. Some students may have generated a table such as the following:

Size of square	Number of squares of that size
4-cm square	1
3-cm square	4
2-cm square	9
1-cm square	16

Total number of squares: 1 + 4 + 9 + 16 = 30

Challenge the students to determine the total number of squares with sides parallel to the sides of a 10 × 10 geoboard. Some students may do this by extending the pattern. [1 + 4 + 9 + 16 + 25 + 36 + 49 + 64 + 81 + 100]

12 × 12 Multiplication Table

1	2	3	4	5	6	7	8	9	10	11	12
2	4	6	8	10	12	14	16	18	20	22	24
3	6	9	12	15	18	21	24	27	30	33	36
4	8	12	16	20	24	28	32	36	40	44	48
5	10	15	20	25	30	35	40	45	50	55	60
6	12	18	24	30	36	42	48	54	60	66	72
7	14	21	28	35	42	49	56	63	70	77	84
8	16	24	32	40	48	56	64	72	80	88	96
9	18	27	36	45	54	63	72	81	90	99	108
10	20	30	40	50	60	70	80	90	100	110	120
11	22	33	44	55	66	77	88	99	110	121	132
12	24	36	48	60	72	84	96	108	120	132	144

Circle Patterns

Choose the number to multiply and complete the multiplication table:

Multiply by _____.

0	1	2	3	4	5	6	7	8	9	10	11	12

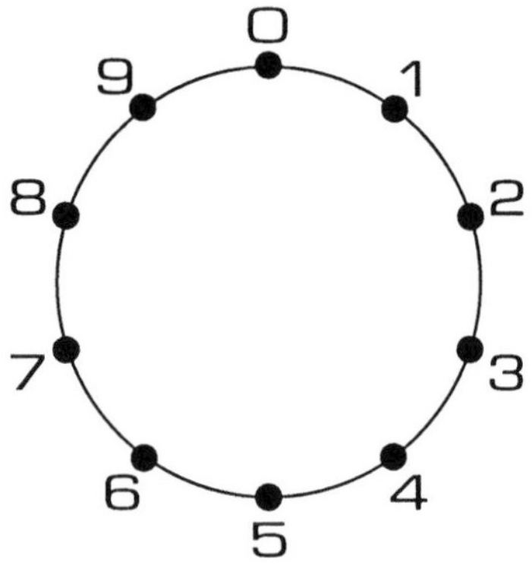

Ring the ones digit in each answer and list the numbers in the pattern.

Use the circle at the right. Connect the numbers in your repeating pattern.

Pattern: _____

Multiply by _____.

0	1	2	3	4	5	6	7	8	9	10	11	12

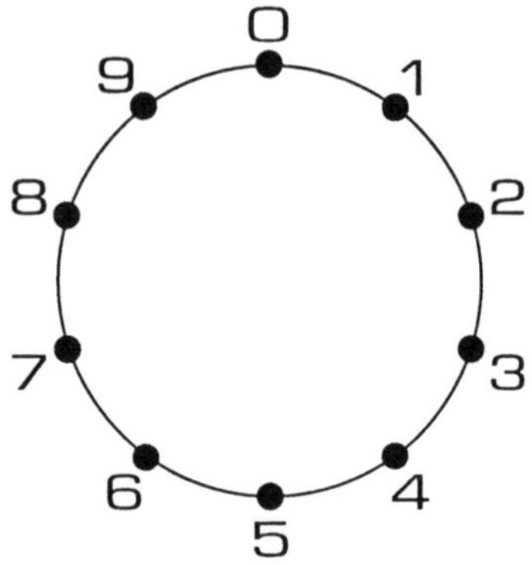

Pattern: _____

Multiply by _____.

0	1	2	3	4	5	6	7	8	9	10	11	12

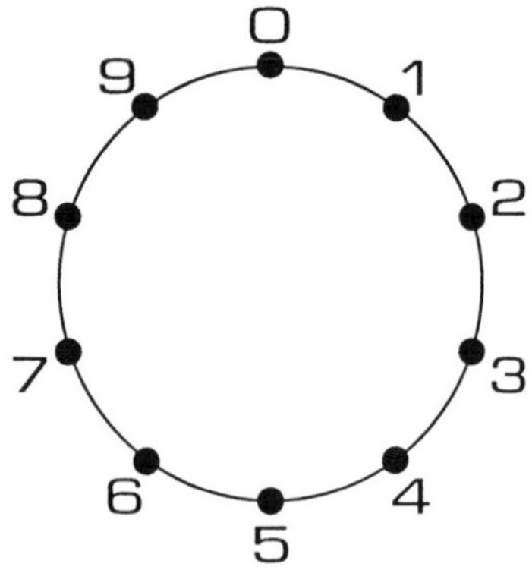

Pattern: _____

Multiply by _____.

0	1	2	3	4	5	6	7	8	9	10	11	12

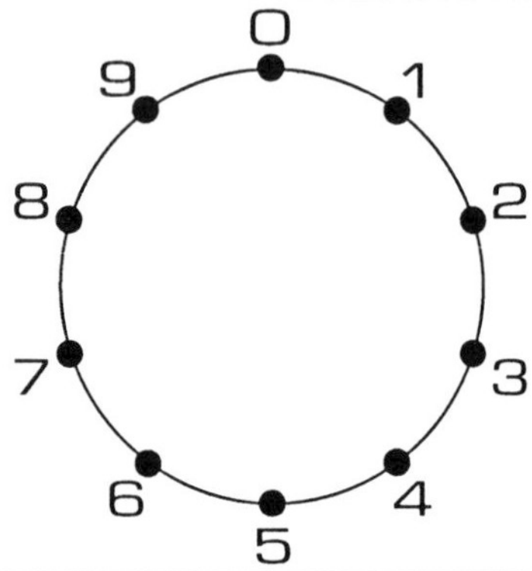

Pattern: _____

NUMBER SENSE AND OPERATIONS

Number sense is the ability to understand and use numbers and operations on numbers in computation, measurement, and estimation situations. This ability takes many years to develop and is well worth the investment; it is valuable to both children and adults as they encounter mathematical situations in and out of school. When children have experiences that encourage them to model and describe numbers in a variety of settings, they will readily learn to apply mathematical understandings in appropriate and efficient ways. It is important to select activities that focus on interesting questions dealing with number and measurement.

In the fourth grade, students typically begin a more intensive study of fractions and decimals. Extending their understanding of whole numbers becomes a major focus of the mathematics program. This section presents a sample of whole and rational number problem-solving activities and illustrates appropriate teaching strategies. For example, you might engage students in short, warm-up activities every day to bring number sense to the fore. In all lessons that involve numbers—in and beyond mathematics—encourage children to use estimation and mental arithmetic whenever feasible. When a calculator is the most appropriate tool, encourage and support its use.

THE QUILT FACTORY

Get ready. The purpose of this activity is to have children apply their knowledge of fractions at concrete and pictorial levels in a creative situation.

Give each student scissors and crayons and several square sheets of plain paper (for part 1) or several sheets of 1″ grid paper (for part 2).

Get going.

Part 1. Describing designs

Ask the students to fold a square to make either two or three equal parts. Have them fold the square again once or twice as suggested by the diagram, which shows an example of three folds. Encourage the children to invent alternative ways of folding.

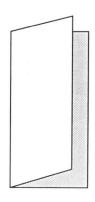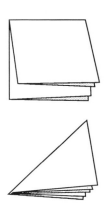

Ask the students to make a design by coloring the parts of the folded square. Have them describe their completed work. Encourage numerical descriptions.

As in the earlier grades, the assessment of students' ability to understand mathematical terms and concepts is best achieved through a natural extension of instructional activities. Such questions as "Why?" "What if?" and "How would you convince someone?" should be asked routinely to help students explain or justify their answers or conjectures. (NCTM 1989a, p. 216)

Students' ability to understand the written and oral communication of others is an important component of instruction and assessment. (NCTM 1989a, p. 214)

The art teacher may wish to work with you in presenting this activity.

How many equal parts did you divide your squares into? What would we call one of these parts? How would you describe your designs by color?

Have the students mount their designs and write about how they created them. Use the designs and reports for a bulletin board display.

Repeat the activity. Once the students have finished coloring, have them describe the design to their partners, who then attempt to duplicate it without seeing the model. Tell the students to use fractional language whenever possible to describe the parts.

Part 2. Replicating quilt patterns

Enlarge one of the quilt designs illustrated below. Suggest that the children copy it onto dot paper, devise a coloring pattern, and decide what part of the design will be a given color. Have them color the quilt pattern and check the fractional amount colored. When the students are ready, have them discuss their artwork and tell how they arrived at each fractional estimate.

You may extend this activity by asking questions such as the following:

Is your design symmetric? How do you know?

How could we group the designs?

If your design were a dart board, what color would you be most likely to hit if you threw one dart? Would a dart be more likely to hit a purple section or a white one? Why?

Keep going. Have each student decide which of the student-designed squares has the largest fraction of a given color. To check, lay a transparent grid over the square. You can make such a grid by running coordinate paper through a transparency maker. This grid will also be handy for demonstrating a particular coloring pattern on the overhead projector.

Ask students to create a design that conforms to given specifications, such as ¼ blue, ¼ blue and green stripe, ½ green. When they finish, ask them to defend their coloring decisions. Encourage the students to use resource materials to discover traditional quilt designs and to discuss why people made quilts from small pieces of material. [Cloth and woven blankets were very expensive. Quilted bed coverings were warm and made good use of the pieces left over from making clothing or snipped from clothing too worn to wear.]

Use the quilt pieces to make a class bulletin board. Construct large group quilts—possibly made from all the designs that fit the same "given specifications"—and hang them on display. Stories describing what was done, giving historical contexts and so on, might accompany the quilts.

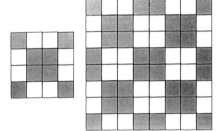

If you choose to make large quilts, you might have students replicate their designs so that they have four congruent designs. Assemble these four pieces into a large square and glue these large squares onto background paper to make several quilts for each class.

As a variation, encourage the students to make a quilt of squares that tell about themselves, such as their hobbies, favorite colors and activities, friends, and so on. Have them describe their personal square.

SPROUTING SEEDS

Get ready. The purpose of this activity is to have students apply fraction concepts in a science setting.

For each team of four students you will need paper towels, four transparent plastic cups, masking tape, sixty seeds (in an envelope) from a bag of birdseed or alfalfa, plastic wrap, and, if possible, a hand lens.

Get going. Discuss germination rates (the fractional part of a group of seeds that is expected to sprout). Furnish each team with the supplies listed above and have them divide the seeds in the envelope so each student in the group has the same number. When the whole team is satisfied that they have completed the task, have each member use the masking tape to label a cup with his or her name. Give the following instructions:

Connections between mathematics and other subjects, such as social studies, enrich both subjects and help students value mathematics.

If students create a design that is 8/16 purple and replicate it three more times, ask what part of the entire 4-block design is purple. Notice that many students count squares, whereas some recognize the relationship between the similar designs.

Extend the science ideas in this lesson to include other factors that affect seed growth.

Counting and predicting lead naturally to topics such as probability and statistics.

Cover the bottom of each cup with a wet paper towel, then place your seeds on the towel. Make a lid from plastic wrap, cover the cup, and put it where it can be observed but remain undisturbed for several days. Make sure that the seeds are kept moist.

When they see the first growth, have the students write their estimates of the fractional part of the seeds they expect to sprout. Show the children that if they expect 10 of their 15 seeds to sprout, they can write ¹⁰⁄₁₅. Remind the students that they are estimating the fractional part that sprouts, not the time it takes to sprout. After the seeds have sprouted, have the students determine the germination rates for their seeds, express the rates as fractions, and compare their estimates to the actual germination rate.

Questions such as "What fractional part of your seeds sprouted?" can be used to guide class discussion. Lay the foundation for the concept of ratio by asking such questions as "Amy had 15 seeds and 10 sprouted. What fractional part of the seeds sprouted and what part did not sprout? If she had 30 seeds how many would she expect to sprout?"

Keep going. A rich variety of activities can grow out of these beginnings. Choose from the following challenges:

♦ Compare the germination rate for various kinds of seeds in a seed mixture.

♦ Find the germination rate across the whole classroom for the different types of seeds. Discuss what students would predict if they were to repeat the experiment (do so if there is time).

♦ Examine commercial seed packets or catalogs to discover the projected germination rates of various seeds. Share these data by means of a graph. If rates are given in percentages, explain that these are sprouting rates for every one hundred seeds.

♦ Sprout such seeds as mung bean, radish, alfalfa, and cabbage (available from health food stores). Conduct a tasting party with the sprouts when they are about five to seven centimeters long.

♦ Measure and graph the growing rates of different seeds under various conditions (sunny window, warm closet, salted water).

HISTORICAL VOYAGES

Get ready. The purpose of this activity is to have children make estimations on the basis of independent readings in science and history.

Get going. Note that people as well as plants need water. Discuss the problem of people at sea who cannot drink the salt water. Pose the following problem:

How much water might Columbus have carried for his trip across the Atlantic? What do you need to know to make an estimate? Where could you start to find this information? Who could help you besides your teacher?

Have the students check reference books for information on the number of people, the length of the trip, the amount of water people need each day, and so on, to make reasoned estimates of the amount of water needed. Discuss how much space would be needed to store the water for the trip.

School mathematics must endow all students with a realization that doing mathematics is a common human activity. Having numerous and varied experiences allows students to trust their own mathematical thinking. (NCTM 1989a, p. 6)

This activity makes connections to history, science, geography, and other areas of mathematics.

Measurement, number sense, and problem solving come together in tasks such as this: Suppose we had to store a week's supply of water in our classroom. Each student needs at least five 8-ounce glasses of water each day. How much water would we need and how would we store it?

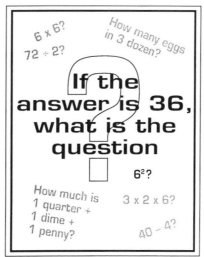

Roald Amundsen

Roald Amundsen from Norway discovered the South Pole in 1906. He had a crew of _____ people and _____ dogs. They planned to be gone for _____ months. They needed _____ kilograms food and _____ liters of water.

Keep going. Solve similar problems involving Marco Polo, Matthew Henson, Charles Lindberg, Amelia Earhart, astronauts going to the moon, and so on. Have each child chose his or her favorite explorer and prepare similar questions for other students to answer.

MINI-MATH MOMENTS—WAYS TO TURN WAITING TIME INTO LEARNING TIME

The Answer Is...

Get ready. The purpose of this activity is to give children mental arithmetic opportunities.

Get going. Announce a number and ask each student in turn to state a question for which that number is the answer. Give the students several examples to encourage nonroutine thinking. ("The answer is 36." Possible questions: "What is 3×12?"; "What is $3 \times 2 \times 6$?"; "How much money is one quarter, one dime, and one penny?"; "What is six more than the number of days in November?"; "What is the number of inches in three feet?") Make large posters for each answer and the questions it generated.

> 6×6?
> $72 \div 2$?
> How many eggs in 3 dozen?
> **If the answer is 36, what is the question** ☐
> 6^2?
> How much is 1 quarter + 1 dime + 1 penny?
> $3 \times 2 \times 6$?
> $40 - 4$?

Encourage the students to record a list of some answers and questions on adding-machine paper. Display the list on parents' night and have visitors add to it.

Keep going. Change the focus from giving many descriptions of a known number to discovering an unknown number, "the answer," through a

Understanding multiple representations for numbers is a crucial precursor to solving many of the problems students encounter. (NCTM 1989a, p. 87)

Depending on the size of the numbers, you can provide calculators for this activity.

Making conjectures, gathering evidence, and building an argument to support such notions are fundamental to doing mathematics. In fact, a demonstration of good reasoning should be rewarded even more than students' ability to find correct answers. (NCTM 1989a, p. 6)

◆　　　◆　　　◆　　　◆　　　◆　　　◆　　　◆　　　◆

series of progressive clues. For example, if "the answer" is 7, you might give the class these clues:

> I am less than 10.
> I am an odd number.
> I am more than 6.
> I am a prime number.

Show the clues one at a time and encourage the students to give possible answers after each clue is uncovered.

After you model several of these "What number am I?" puzzles, have the students write their own for others to solve. You may wish to give them guidelines, such as the riddles must have at least four clues but no more than seven clues or the riddles should have two possible answers.

Make It More, Make It Less

Get ready. The purpose of this activity is to have students use their knowledge of number and place value in mental arithmetic.

Each pair of students will need a number cube labeled 1 through 6.

Get going. The purpose of the game is to reach either 0 or 100 by deciding what operation to use on each successive randomly generated number. Pair the students and have each student begin by writing down 50. To play, the first student rolls the number cube, decides whether to add, subtract, multiply, or divide the two numbers (the number rolled and the number written), performs the operation, and records the result on his or her paper. Then it is the second student's turn. Play continues until one partner reaches either 100 or 0.

What operation might this student choose in round 4?

Beginning number	Number rolled	Operation	Ending number
50	6	–	44
44	4	÷	11
11	5	–	6
6	2	?	?

Keep going. An option is to use two or more number cubes and allow a combination of operations. You can also use number cubes marked 10 through 60, a starting point of 500, and a goal of 1000 or 0.

For a whole-class activity, roll a number cube ten times. For each roll, each student must decide to multiply the number rolled by 1, 10, or 100 and then sum the ten products. The student whose sum is closest to 1000 is the winner.

My birthday is 2/25/82.
My favorite numbers are 7 and 12.
$\frac{2}{2} + 5 + 8 - 2 = 12$
$22 - 5 - 8 - 2 = 7$

Ryan

Dateline

Get ready. The purposes of this activity are to have students discover different ways to express a given number and to reinforce the order of operations.

Get going. Using this format, write the date 1/8/91. Have the students use any operations desired and those four digits arranged in any order to arrive at a given target number, such as 1. (Example: $1 + 9 - 8 - 1 = 1$) Have the students write their solutions on the overhead projector or on the chalkboard.

Keep going. Develop a similar activity by using many other sets of digits, such as four 4s, five 5s, someone's birth date, or the digits of the year.

Challenge the students to use the digits 1, 2, 3, 4, 5, 6, 7, 8, and 9, in that order, with any operation sign to reach 100. For example, 123 – 4 – 5 – 6 – 7 + 8 – 9 = 100.

Can you find another solution? Do you think there are more?

Challenge another class to find more solutions. Post the latest solution along with the student's picture on your door.

Fill It Up

Get ready. The purpose of this activity is to have students practice written computation that emphasizes knowledge of place value and strategic thinking.

You need slips of paper or disks numbered 0 through 9 and a bag from which to draw them.

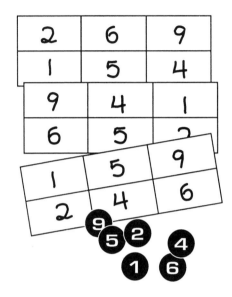

Get going. Have the students draw a 2 × 3 array on their paper.

Tell them that you will draw a disk from the bag and call out the number. As they hear the number, they must write it in one of the six rectangles. Once they write the number, they cannot move it. You will draw a disk in this way six times, replacing the disk in the bag after each selection.

When six numbers have been called and all the children have added together the two three-digit numbers they have created, call on one child to give his or her sum.

Did anyone get a higher sum?

Have a student explain how he or she got it.

Is there a still higher sum? Is there another way to get that sum?

What is the lowest sum you could get with these six numbers? In how many ways can you get that sum?

If we use a 3 × 2 array instead of the 2 × 3 array, will you change your strategy? How? Which array will yield larger sums? Why?

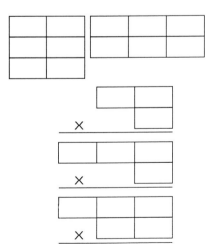

Keep going. You may vary this activity as follows:

- Do not replace the disks after selecting each one. Ask the students how that will change their strategy.
- Draw seven disks; players may erase and replace exactly one number.
- Use a 3 × 2 array or a 2 × 4 array.
- Have the children subtract the numbers. The goal is to get the largest difference.
- Have the children subtract the numbers. The goal is to get the difference closest to zero.
- Have the students draw two boxes over one box to create a format for multiplication.
- Where should I put the largest number to get the largest product?
- Challenge them to extend their results to other numbers of digits. You may wish to allow the students to use calculators.
- Use a format for division with a one-digit divisor and a four-digit dividend.

Lead the students in discussing the different strategies they used for the different operations. Use calculators to explore the same activity with decimals. See if the strategies are different using decimals.

Computer software also is a significant component of a comprehensive problem-solving program. Many excellent software packages enable children to develop and apply problem-solving strategies in geometry, logical reasoning, classification, measurement, fractions and decimals, and other mathematical content. (NCTM 1989a, p. 24)

In Logo, an on-screen "turtle" responds to instructions to draw geometric figures.

FORWARD 50 (or FD 50) instructs the turtle to move forward 50 "turtle steps" in whatever direction it is pointing. Other commands include the following:

RIGHT 90 (RT 90): Rotate 90 degrees to the right.

PENUP (PU): Put the pen up, so that a path is not drawn.

PENDOWN (PD): Put the pen down, so that a path is drawn.

HT hides the turtle.

ST shows the turtle.

Commands to clear the screen differ; try CS, DRAW, or CG.

It is important that children connect ideas both among and within areas of mathematics. (NCTM 1989a, p. 32)

COMPUTER COUNTERS

Get ready. The purpose of this activity is to have students use their knowledge of place value in estimation. Use a computer with the Logo language as a counter.

How long do you think it will take John to count to 1000? Write down your estimate.

Ask John to count to 100.

Would you change your estimate? Why or why not?

Time John's count to 1000 and ask the students to discuss the accuracy of their estimates.

Get going. Assign the children to groups according to the number of computers available. Choose one child to be the keyboard operator in each group. Have the student clear the screen and key in the following commands (if you wish, define them as a procedure).

    MAKE "COUNT 0
    REPEAT 100 [MAKE "COUNT :COUNT + 1 PRINT :COUNT]

These commands will make the computer count to 100. As the computer counts, the group should time it carefully with a clock and record how long the count took. Then change REPEAT 100 to REPEAT 1000. Have the students estimate how long the computer will now take.

Was your estimate close or not close?

Ask the students how they arrived at that number. Then change the target number to 2000 and have them make and verify new estimates.

When the children are comfortable with the procedure, tell them to estimate how long it would take the computer to count to 10 000 and to give reasons for their answer.

Keep going. Ask the students what commands would make the computer count by 10s to 1000.

    MAKE "COUNT 0
    REPEAT 100 [MAKE "COUNT :COUNT + 10 PRINT :COUNT]

Have the children decide how long it would take to count by 2s or 5s to a target number such as 100.

The following counting problems may interest your students:

If you stacked $10.00 worth of pennies, how tall would the stack be? How many pennies would be in the stack?

How many pennies are in $100.00? Could you carry them at one time?

MAKING SENSE OF DATA

Fourth grade is a wonderful time for children to see the connections among their school subjects. There is no better way to do this than by making sense of all the information around them. They can use the techniques of collecting, analyzing, and presenting data in many situations that arise from various subject areas.

In this set of activities, the children collect data by making measurements. In so doing, they explore ideas from science, mathematics, and social studies. As they talk and write about their findings, they use their language art skills. As they listen to other children, they learn from each other.

Statistics and probability are important links to other content areas, such as social studies and science. They also can reinforce communication skills as children discuss and write about their activities and their conclusions. Within mathematics, these topics regularly involve the uses of number, measurement, estimation, and problem solving. (NCTM 1989a, p. 54)

Children often have the idea that measurement results in an exact number. The experiments in this set of activities help children understand that all measurements are approximate and that it is often wise to take several measurements of the same phenomenon.

As with all suggestions in this book, these activities do not attempt to develop all the necessary concepts or skills associated with making sense of data. They do provide springboards for further investigations. If children develop the spirit of inquiry and discover ways to organize and analyze information, they will have the ability to continue learning and using their knowledge. You will notice a difference in how they approach their work if you give them many opportunities to make decisions about sets of information.

How do you know which children are beginning to delve beyond the obvious information displayed in their graphs? Logs or journals in which students record their thoughts throughout the process are valuable sources for evaluation. Another source is students' responses to thought-provoking questions. "If you were going to do a similar study again, what would you do differently and why? How could you improve your project?"

Children often view mathematics as a subject that can be done quickly and exactly. This long-term project is one way to help children see that much of mathematics takes time and that often the answers are not exact.

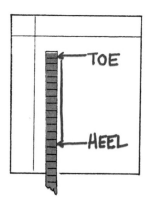

It is good for the students to be responsible for carrying out tasks on their own or with a friend. This independence helps build their confidence in their ability to do mathematics, a goal of the Curriculum and Evaluation Standards for School Mathematics *(NCTM 1989a).*

OH, HOW WE'VE CHANGED!

Get ready. The purposes of this activity are to have students collect data over time and analyze data in a variety of ways.

Children will need metric rulers and measuring tape to measure monthly their height in centimeters and the length of their feet in millimeters. They record their findings on a copy of Oh, How I've Changed! (p. 22).

Get going. At the beginning of the school year, pose this question to your students:

How many centimeters in all do you think our class will grow during the year?

Discuss with the class why the question is not clear—they grow in height, in the distance around their waists, in the length of their feet, and so forth. Tell the children that you were thinking of their height and the length of their feet. You may wish to have an estimation contest in which the students guess how much the class will grow in each of these areas.

Give each child a copy of Oh, How I've Changed! and help the class fill in the information for September.

The children may need help determining their age in years and months. To measure heights easily, attach to the wall a centimeter tape or a strip of adding-machine tape marked every ten centimeters. Decide on a common way to measure feet to the nearest millimeter. The children might mark the back of their right heel and the tip of their big toe on paper and then measure the distance between the marks as shown.

Begin class graphs of the *growth* in height and in foot length for the year and for each month. Because you will be focusing only on growth, begin each person at zero. See the sample of the graph for feet that shows growth in October. When the children get used to measuring, they can do this activity independently during the first week of each month and record their growth on the monthly bar graphs.

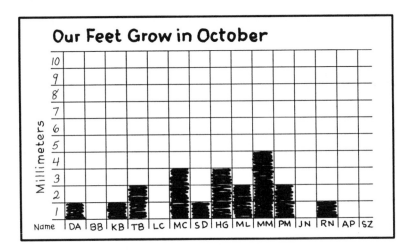

Keep the interest going through the months by having someone total the number of centimeters and the number of millimeters each month. If you are having an estimation contest, let the children change their estimates in December and March and talk about why they changed the estimates as they did. At the end of the school year, calculate the total change for the year for each child.

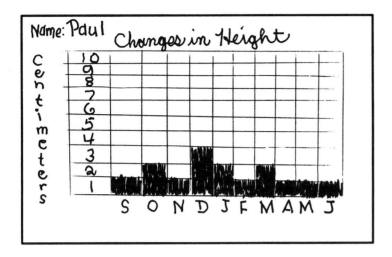

Students can also keep individual data sheets to record or graph their own growth and to make personal comparisons throughout the year.

Keep going. At the end of the year, use this activity as a rich source of further investigations and as a culmination of what the children learned in fourth grade:

Did the boys grow more in height than the girls?

Did the girls' feet grow more than the boys' feet?

Did people with brown eyes grow more than people with blue eyes or green eyes?

Did people with blond hair grow more than people with other hair colors?

Did people who were below the class mean [average] in height in September grow more than people who were above the class mean?

In which month was there more growth in height?

Did older or younger children grow more?

For students who enter your class after September, estimate their measurements as of September so that they can participate fully. The class may wish to help make this estimate.

Your students may think of other questions that they wish to answer, especially after looking at the graphs. Have small groups of students each work on one question using the original data. If necessary, model how to transfer the data from the original source so that students can use it easily. For example, if they are examining the color of hair and the height, they could make a column for each color and under it write the growth in height for each person with that color hair. After they have had time to organize and analyze the data, they should present it to the class. They may want to make new graphs to support their conclusions.

As an extension, the students might design a study to survey adults' ability to estimate how long a meter is. How many adults give estimates that are too long, too short, or just about right? The students need to define these categories.

HOW FAR AND WHY?

Get ready. The purpose of this activity is to have children collect data in an experiment. They examine the variables that might cause a change in the distance a ball will travel when rolled through a tube.

You will need at least one marble, one tube such as a paper towel tube, a ruler, and a meter stick for each small group, as well as an area for rolling the marble through the tube and onto the floor or the ground. If different sizes of marbles (or small balls) and different lengths of tubes are available, the children will have more to investigate. An alternative is to use toy cars and ramps.

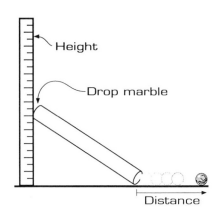

Height

Drop marble

Distance

| Height of tube | Three measurements | | | Average |
	1	2	3	
0 cm				
5 cm				
10 cm	103	99	97	100
15 cm				
20 cm				
25 cm				
30 cm				

One teacher reported that all her students were using a paper towel tube and the same-size marble. They raised questions about the length of the tube, the size of the marble, the type of floor, and the diameter of the tube. This led to a whole series of experiments. Help your students develop that type of thinking: "What if we...?"

Get going. Place one end of a tube on the floor and the other end against a ruler held perpendicular to the floor. Show the students how to measure the height of the upper end of the tube and where to drop the marble (see illustration). Ask them to predict the height that will make the marble roll the longest distance. Someone should note that the ball will not roll if the tube is lying flat or if the tube is upright. The students' job is to find out which position will give the longest roll.

Have each group make three rolls at each height they decide to try. They should record these data along with the height of the tube on a chart such as that shown at the left.

They then should discuss the range of numbers and decide which one of these three measurements would best describe the roll at each height. It may be the average (mean) or the median (the middle number when ordered least to greatest) or the best of the three rolls. Have the students graph the results with a broken line graph by using the height of the tube along the x-axis and the distance of the roll along the y-axis.

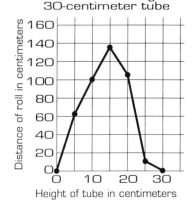

Marble roll through a 30-centimeter tube

When the children have completed all the graphs, have them look at the results. Help them wrestle with the following questions:

What do you notice that is similar in all the graphs?

Are there differences? What may have caused the differences?

If the children have not come up with other questions, encourage this type of thinking by asking questions such as these:

What would happen if the tube were twice as long or twice as wide?

Would a larger marble roll farther?

What would happen if we rolled a toy truck down a ramp? Would it matter if it were loaded?

The children can carry out other experiments on their own to answer some of these questions.

Keep going. Comparing the bounce heights of a tennis ball and a golf ball is a worthwhile extension. The tennis ball will bounce higher than the golf ball when dropped from certain heights. As the height increases, however, the golf ball begins to bounce higher in relation to the tennis ball and finally surpasses it.

Look for other experiments involving length. Science and physical education programs are a good source of ideas. For example: How far do different designs of paper airplanes fly? Why? How far can each student jump?

WHICH PAPER TOWEL GETS THE WETTEST?

Get ready. The purpose of this activity is to have students experiment with the amount of area covered by water drops on different types of paper towels or other absorbent papers. In so doing, they will be posing questions, organizing the experiment, collecting the data, and analyzing and reporting the results.

Each group of children will need water (several different colors dyed with tempera paint or food coloring, although they can use clear water), a dropper or a small measuring spoon, an assortment of paper towels or napkins (children can bring several sheets from home to get variety or you can collect paper from around the school—newspapers, napkins, paper towels, and so on), and a transparent square-centimeter grid. The groups can share the dropper or the measuring spoon.

Get going. Discuss advertisements that claim a certain brand of paper towel is most absorbent. Pose the question of how much area would be covered by water if one-eighth teaspoon or four drops were dropped on a paper towel. Most likely the students will have no idea at this point. Continue the conversation by asking such questions as these:

Will the type of paper towel make a difference?

If you use twice as much water, will it cover twice as much paper?

If you fold the paper in half, will the water cover twice as much area?

Let the groups decide on the question or questions that they would like to answer about the area of the shapes covered with water. The children may need to do some free experimenting before they decide on a prediction that they would like to make. They should design their experiment to convince themselves and others that their prediction was right or wrong.

Suggest that they use a different color water for different variables, such as red for five drops of water, blue for ten drops of water, and so on. Also suggest that they dry off the surface after dropping the water on one sheet so that the next sheet won't pick up old water.

If the children have previously found approximate areas of odd shapes by placing a clear grid over the shape or by placing the shape on a piece of graph paper, they may gravitate to one of those procedures. If not, be ready to help children assign a number to the area by using the grids and counting the squares.

5 drops
about 54 squares

10 drops

As in the previous activity, encourage the students to make each measurement three times. When they have gathered the data and decided what the data mean, have them write a brief report to give to the class. It may be appropriate for some groups to make a graph; others may only need to discuss the measurements and the results.

Keep going. Each group could take a brand of paper towels and try to convince others that their brand is the best (best being defined by the manufacturer or the consumer; they must decide). There are many other ways that children can measure a paper towel. They may wish to see which towel will hold the most weight (use pennies, washers, or other weights) when it is wet. Others may want to measure the thickness (put several sheets together to do this), the size of each sheet, or the cost for each sheet.

Children can see the usefulness of measurement if classroom experiences focus on measuring real objects, making objects of given sizes, and estimating measurements. Textbook experiences cannot substitute for activities that use measurement to answer questions about real problems. (NCTM 1989a, p. 53)

Children of this age will naturally put parts of squares together to make another square when approximating the area. They may need some assistance in keeping track of the counted squares. Let the children decide on the method and share with others how to use it. As children make decisions, the method they use will make sense to them even though it may not be the most efficient way.

Discussions reveal students' understandings. For example, what does it mean when one paper towel shows a larger wet area? Is it more absorbent (students may believe "it's soaking up the water better") or less absorbent ("it takes a smaller area of the towel to absorb the same amount of water")?

Oh, How I've Changed!

Name _____

Color of eyes _____

Color of hair _____

Age in September: Years _____   Months _____

	Height in centimeters	Length of foot in mm	Your choice _____
Sept.			
Oct.			
Nov.			
Dec.			
Jan.			
Feb.			
Mar.			
Apr.			
May			
June			

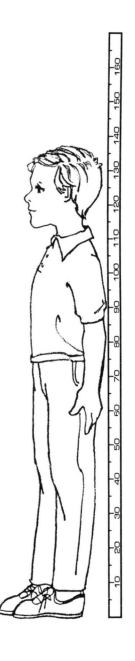

GEOMETRY AND SPATIAL SENSE

Geometry activities are valuable because they not only develop spatial and geometric ideas but also promote exploration and reasoning. If geometric ideas emerge from the children's physical world, then geometry is both practically useful and aesthetically satisfying.

Connections among geometry, spatial sense, and other areas of mathematics should continue throughout a student's experiences. For example, one activity here is related to conservation of area through the use of flips and turns and visualization.

The use of manipulatives remains important at the fourth-grade level in enriching and extending children's experiences. The computer also allows children to manipulate geometric ideas but in a way that helps connect the concrete to the abstract. In these activities, children "act out" or "walk through" the steps and turns that an on-screen "turtle" would take in moving around a geometric figure. Some of you will be venturing into unfamiliar territory when using computers, but you will be pleasantly surprised at the number of spatial abilities that are employed and are necessary for success.

EXPLORING RIGHT ANGLES

Get ready. The purposes of this activity are to have children internalize the concept of right angle, make a right-angle corner, and find right angles in the environment.

Right angles are common in the environment and in materials that students use every day in the classroom. Give children an opportunity to discover right angles in objects they see around them. Turning is a natural physical movement that you can use to help students develop the initial concept of angle.

The right-angle turn is used extensively in Logo programs. The command RT 90 means turn right through 90°. The command LT 90 means turn left through 90°. Physically, these are quarter-turns. RT 180 and LT 180 are half-turns.

Materials needed for this activity are geoboards, geopaper, scrap paper, and models of solids. Some extensions of this activity call for a computer with the Logo computer language. If computers are unavailable, these extensions can be conducted without a computer, by students pretending to be a "turtle" and following the Logo commands.

Get going. *How could you describe a square corner? How could you fold a piece of paper of any shape to make a square corner?*

Discuss the solution shown. The first fold is a straight line. The second fold makes a square corner—that is, the two folds form a square corner.

Have the children use their square corner to find objects in the classroom that contain a square corner and those that have angles that measure less than or more than a square corner.

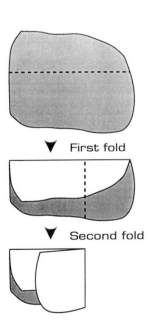

▼ First fold

▼ Second fold

These types of questions can be adapted to activity cards for a mathematics center. Children can make up similar problems to add to the set.

Tell the children that another name for *square corner* is *right angle*. Have the children draw two lines that they think are at right angles and check them by using their square corners.

Have them draw angles less than or greater than right angles.

Draw angles for the children that are "almost" right angles and ask them to judge visually whether each angle is less than or greater than a right angle. Check with a square corner.

How many right angles does a square have? How many does a rectangle have?

Show the children several solids, such as those pictured.

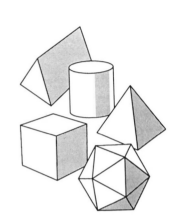

Which of these solid figures have square corners on their faces? [Cube and triangular prism.] *How many right angles does each have?* [The cube has 24, 4 on each of 6 faces; the prism has 12, 4 on each of 3 faces.]

How many angles that are greater than a right angle does each solid have on its faces? How many angles that are less than a right angle?

Explore other solids. Are there any with no square corners?

These problems involve precision in language as well as knowledge of "right angle." For example, all figures above have "one right angle"—that is, at least one—but some figures have "just one right angle."

Have the children use a 5 × 5 geoboard to construct figures having—

just one right angle;

at least one right angle;

exactly two right angles;

six right angles;

no right angles;

three right angles and seven sides;

as many right angles as they can make.

Possible answers

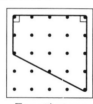

| Just one right angle | Exactly two right angles |

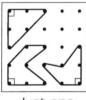

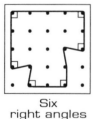

Six right angles

These problems have a variety of solutions. Children may become interested in trying to find as many as they can.

Several answers are possible for some of the problems. Have the children compare their geoboard solutions. Another way to record solutions for all to see is with loops of string and pushpins on the bulletin board. In this situation, the children must estimate the right angles (or use their square corners).

Show the children a 3 × 3 grid representing a map of city blocks. Have them draw a path that a taxicab could take from A to B.

How many right angles are in your path?

Possible answers

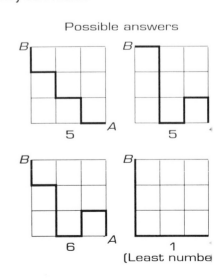

The children can record their answers on grid paper or geopaper. Those children who have difficulty identifying all the right angles could walk along a grid on the floor. (Use chalk or masking tape to make a grid.) Each right or left turn will indicate a square corner. Have the children design other pathways for the taxicab, with five square corners, with six square corners, with the greatest number of square corners, and with the least number of square corners. (Children may raise the question, "Is retracing a part of the path allowed?")

Using a computer with the Logo computer language, show the children how to make the turtle draw a square to represent the outline of the "city blocks."

If each side of the large square is 75 turtle steps long, how many steps FORWARD would I have the turtle move to go one-third of the way up the square? [25]

(If computer facilities are not available, outline the grid on the floor with tape or on the playground with chalk. Have one child act as the "turtle" while another gives instructions.)

What Logo commands would take the turtle from the lower right (A) corner to the upper left (B) corner while keeping the turtle on the imaginary grid? (See the "Instructions to make a path" for one solution.)

Challenge the children to write Logo commands for a different route the turtle could take in going from A to B while staying on the imaginary grid.

What was your solution? How many right angles did this route have? Could we find all the possible solutions?

Keep going. Explain to the children that the surface of water in a tank is horizontal and a string attached to a heavy object is vertical. (This is how *horizontal* and *vertical* are defined.)

How are the directions vertical and horizontal related? [They are at right angles to one another.]

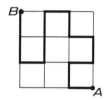

Horizontal   Vertical

Look for objects or parts of objects in the room that are vertical and objects that are horizontal.

How would you determine that you are standing at right angles to the floor? What difficulty might you have if you were not standing at right angles to the floor? [It would be difficult to stand.]

Why do you think that walls are built at right angles to the ground? [They would tend to fall over otherwise.]

Ask the children to look for buildings in the neighborhood (or in photos or books) that have walls that are not vertical, and discuss possible reasons for this. [Some modern architecture, tents, roof lines]

What would the world be like if all the right angles in objects suddenly disappeared? Explore the question through discussion, writing, drawing, or model building.

Instructions to make the square:

TO SQUARE
FD 75
LT 90
FD 75
LT 90
FD 75
LT 90
FD 75
LT 90
END

Instructions to make a path:

FD 25
LT 90
FD 25
RT 90
FD 25
LT 90
FD 50
RT 90
FD 25

A different route:

LT 90
FD 25
RT 90
FD 25
RT 90
FD 25
LT 90
FD 25
LT 90
FD 25
RT 90
FD 25
LT 90
FD 25
LT 90
FD 50
RT 90
FD 25
RT 90
FD 50

Students will enjoy learning about the Tower of Pisa and what engineers are predicting about its future.

A way to make the largest possible square:

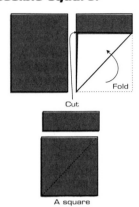

Fold

Cut

A square

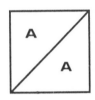

When the square is cut apart and the pieces are rearranged to make a triangle or a parallelogram, the area remains the same. Children may not be aware of this connection, which could be explored through class discussion. You could also examine the perimeters to see if they are the same by representing each perimeter with a piece of string and then comparing the lengths of the strings.

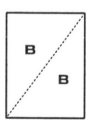

FIGURE ASSEMBLY

Get ready. The purpose of this activity is to have children "examine the result of combining two shapes to form a new shape...[so as to] acquire a deeper understanding of shapes and their properties" (NCTM 1989a, p. 49).

This activity promotes spatial sense—the child must first cut a geometric figure into two parts that have the same size and shape and then mentally manipulate the parts, reassembling them to form other specific figures. Both visualization and visual memory are involved, since the child must retain a visual image of the required final figure while manipulating the parts.

Materials needed for this activity are sheets of 8½″ × 11″ paper or graph paper (two for each child or pair of children) and scissors. Pattern blocks and triangle dot paper are used for the extensions.

Get going. Ask the children to fold a rectangular sheet of 8½″ × 11″ paper to make a square. Illustrate if necessary.

How do you know it is a square? (The reasons may deal with equal side lengths, matching angles, right angles, or lines of symmetry.)

Have the children cut the square along the diagonal (the fold line) to make two triangles. The children should be able to demonstrate that the two triangles have the same shape and the same size by fitting one on top of the other. The teacher may wish to use the term *congruent* to describe the relationship between the two triangles. Label each triangle "A" for future reference.

Have the children rearrange the two triangles to make—

one larger triangle;

a parallelogram;

the original square.

Give another sheet of 8½″ × 11″ paper to each student or pair of students. Have them fold the paper on a diagonal. Point out that one triangle does not fit exactly on the other. The diagonal of a rectangle is not a line of symmetry. Have the students cut along a diagonal to make two triangles. Compare the two triangles just cut.

Are they congruent? Do they have the same area? Label each new triangle "B." Compare a B triangle with an A triangle. How are they alike? How are they different?

Challenge the children to rearrange the two B triangles to form—

a triangle (two ways);

a parallelogram (two ways, not including the original rectangle);

a kite;

the original rectangle.

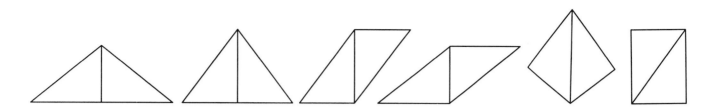

How did you move the triangles to make each figure?

Guide the children's first responses so they see that neither triangle can be made unless one of the original pieces is turned over (flipped); the parallelograms and the rectangle may be assembled without turning or flipping the pieces (slide only).

Use one triangle A and one triangle B to make a triangle with no two sides equal.

Compare all triangles that have been made by combining the A and the B triangles. Discuss the differences in sizes (height, width, area) and the fact that some are isosceles (have two sides the same length) and some are not.

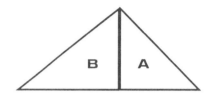

When students talk about the figures you will be able to observe those who use appropriate geometric terms as a natural part of conversation and those who describe spatial relationships correctly.

Keep going. Use pattern blocks or sets of figures cut out of heavy paper for these activities. The answers provided are just samples; there may be many possible solutions.

Challenge the students to use four triangles from the pattern blocks to make—

a large triangle;

a four-sided figure;

a six-sided figure.

Is it possible to make a figure (using four triangles) that has five sides? Seven sides? Eight sides? What is the greatest number of sides possible?

What if the triangles need not touch along whole sides?

If four pattern block triangles are placed so that whenever two triangles touch they touch along a whole side, how many different (noncongruent) arrangements of the four triangles are possible?

Extend this question to figures made with five triangular pattern blocks.

Ask the children to choose a different pattern block shape, use four of these shapes to make other figures, and record their results on triangle dot paper.

Children can cut paper shapes and make new shapes from the parts. (NCTM 1989a, p. 49)

Seven sides

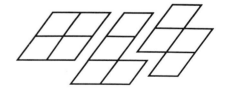

FIGURES AND THEIR SHADOWS

Get ready. The purpose of this activity is to give children experiences in recognizing geometric figures in a variety of sizes and positions in space by making shadows of the geometric figures. This spatial ability is called *perceptual constancy.*

Light and shadow provide the brain with valuable cues to angles, curvature, and depth. For example, astronomers have deduced the shape and the size of mountains on the moon by studying their shadows.

Observing objects and their shadows is an everyday experience for children. As a real-world application, children can explore both expected and unexpected shadows produced by familiar geometric figures.

Materials needed are plane figures and solids that are commonly found in the classroom, pencils or straws, tape, and a strong light source (lamp, flashlight, projector, or bright sunlight).

Get going. Discuss hand shadows that children may have made. Show them a cut-out square taped to a pencil or a straw.

What shadow shapes do you think I could make from this square?

Using the same square, challenge the students to create shadows that are shaped like a square, a rectangle, and a line segment.

What did you do to make each shadow shape?

Can you create any other shadow shapes by using a square?

Have the students explore what happens when they hold the square at various angles to the beam of light.

If this is used in an activity center, children can record their findings by making shadows on plain paper and tracing around them.

Have the children explore possible shadow shapes by using plane figures such as rectangles, triangles of many shapes, squares, regular hexagons, and circles.

Have them explore possible shadow shapes by using solids such as cubes, cylinders, cones, rectangular prisms, and different pyramids. A

◆　　◆　　◆　　◆　　◆　　◆　　◆　　◆

cube, for example, can produce a shadow shaped like a square, a rectangle, or even a hexagon. A cylinder's shadow might be a circle, an oval, or a rectangle.

Plane figures can give a shadow shaped like a line segment but three-dimensional figures cannot. Ask the children to explain why this is so.

Keep going. Have the children place a stick upright in the ground on a bright sunny day around 9:00 a.m.

When mathematical ideas are also connected to every-day experiences, both in and out of school, children be-come aware of the useful-ness of mathematics. (NCTM 1989a, p. 32)

Each half-hour, mark on the ground the end of the shadow cast by the stick. Note how the shadow has turned each half-hour.

Compare the shadow length at 12:00 noon with the shadows at other times.

Why is the shadow shortest at noon?

Explore the speed of the end of the shadow at times before and after noon by comparing distances between the marks.

Why is it faster earlier and later than at noon? Why are the marks not equally spaced?

How could you use this shadow method to make a clock?

Have the children research such topics as sundials, clocks, and time. They may wish to design an original clock as a class project.

The K–4 program is rich with opportunities to use mathematics in other sub-ject areas....This is especial-ly true with science. (NCTM 1989a, p. 35)

The power of computers also needs to be used in contemporary mathematics programs. Computer languages that are geometric in nature help young children become familiar with important geometric ideas. (NCTM 1989a, p. 19)

LOGO AND SYMMETRIC FIGURES

Get ready. The purpose of this activity is to have children compare the paths a Logo turtle traverses around the two figures formed by dividing squares, rectangles, and equilateral triangles along a line of symmetry.

Technology cannot replace active instruction and exploration with physical objects because the development of concepts relies, to a great extent, on the manipulation of concrete objects. Logo can help in the transition from concrete experiences with geometric ideas to abstract reasoning. Activities involving the computer should not stand alone.

Students should know that a line of symmetry of a figure can be illustrated or identified by folding a figure onto itself. A rectangle has two lines of symmetry, a square has four, and an equilateral triangle has three.

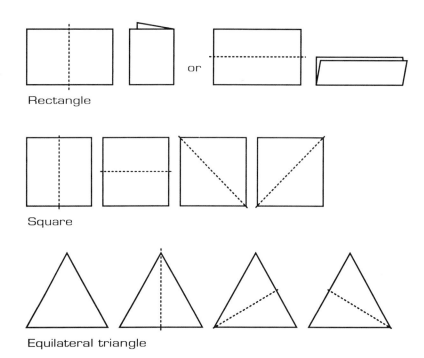

Rectangle

Square

Equilateral triangle

For this set of activities, students need to know measures of 45°, 90°, 120°, and 135° and the meaning of turning in a clockwise or counterclockwise direction. In addition, they should recall the Logo commands of RT (right), LT (left), FD (forward), PU (pen up), and PD (pen down). A new command is HOME—the turtle moves to its starting place. A set of Logo commands that outlines a procedure is called a program. In the first activity, the rectangle is 120 "turtle steps" long and 40 "turtle steps" wide. The program that takes the turtle from *A* to *B* in one direction is compared with the program that takes the turtle from *A* to *B* in the other direction. If a computer is not available, have the children act out the motions of the turtle.

Get going. The teacher should copy the program and the diagram at the left onto an overhead transparency. (The old reliable chalkboard will also suffice.) Tell the children that the turtle starts at *A* and moves around the right half of the rectangle first. The direction around is called counterclockwise (the opposite way the hands of a clock move). In all programs, the turtle starts by facing up the page. Point out that the first command gets the turtle going in the right direction.

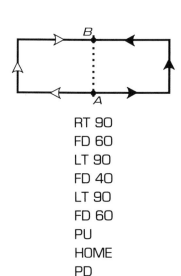

RT 90
FD 60
LT 90
FD 40
LT 90
FD 60
PU
HOME
PD

Have the children write a Logo program that takes the turtle from *A* to *B* in a clockwise direction. The turtle should reappear at *A*.

Compare the two programs. How are they the same? [FD 60 and FD 40 commands are the same.]

How are they different? [Each RT 90 command is replaced by LT 90 and the reverse.]

Copy the incomplete program and the diagram at the right on an over-head transparency or on the chalkboard.Tell the children that the turtle is to start at *A*, move around the left half of the rectangle to *B*, and reappear at *A*. Remind them that the turtle faces up the page to start. The complete rectangle has a height of 90 turtle steps and a width of 60 turtle steps. Work with the children to fill in the blanks.

If a computer is available, have the children clear the screen, then use the commands just given to draw half the figure.

Write a program to draw the other half of the rectangle (the right side). Compare the two programs. [The FD commands remain the same; the LT and RT commands are interchanged.]

Draw a square on the overhead projector or on the chalkboard.

Have the class recall that a diagonal of a square is a line of symmetry. You may wish to demonstrate by paper folding.

You have been given an incomplete program in which the turtle moves from A to B, reappears at A, and draws the left half of a square with sides 40 turtle steps long. What does the first command, LT 45, mean? [A quarter-turn]

Complete the Logo program, visualize the other half of the square, and write a program that will make the turtle move from A to B and reappear at A to complete the other half of the square.

Keep going. *You have been given an incomplete set of commands for drawing an equilateral triangle that is symmetric about the dotted line. Clear the screen and write a complete set of commands for each half of the triangle. Start at A for each half.*

Help the students determine the distance from C to B. Recall that the line of symmetry AB cuts the base of the triangle into two equal parts. FD 20 tells us that the length of AC is 20 steps. The base of the triangle is 40. Since the triangle is equilateral, all the sides must be 40 steps long.

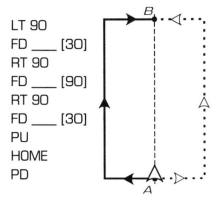

LT 90
FD ____ [30]
RT 90
FD ____ [90]
RT 90
FD ____ [30]
PU
HOME
PD

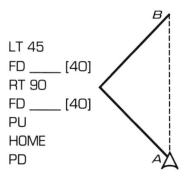

LT 45
FD ____ [40]
RT 90
FD ____ [40]
PU
HOME
PD

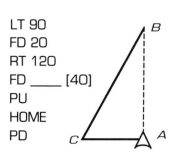

LT 90
FD 20
RT 120
FD ____ [40]
PU
HOME
PD

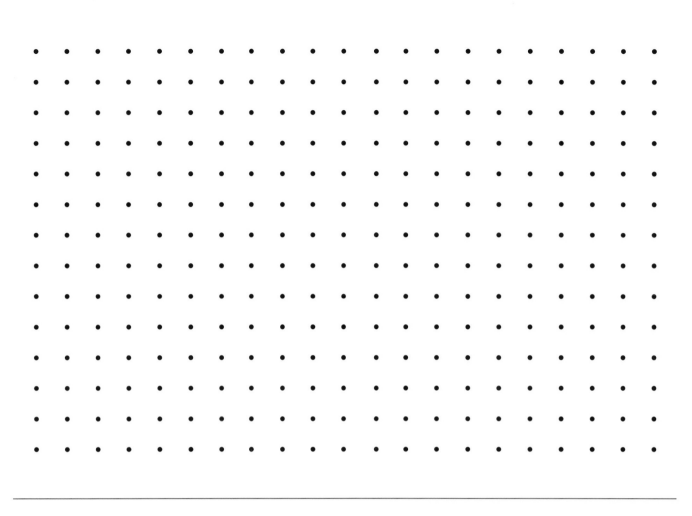